The New Americans
Colonial Times • 1620-1689

◆

Betsy Maestro

◆

Illustrated by Giulio Maestro

LOTHROP, LEE & SHEPARD BOOKS • MORROW

NEW YORK

W9-DIF-429

For Susan Pearson

Note: Not all Native American groups could be included
on the maps in this book. Many of the names have
alternative spellings, and locations are not exact,
as many groups moved from place to place.

The illustrations in this book were done in watercolor
and colored pencil on illustration board.
The text type is 14-point ITC Garamond Book.

Text copyright © 1998 by Betsy Maestro
Illustrations copyright © 1998 by Giulio Maestro

Published by Lothrop, Lee & Shepard Books
an imprint of Morrow Junior Books
a division of William Morrow and Company, Inc.
1350 Avenue of the Americas, New York, NY 10019
www.williammorrow.com

Printed in Singapore at Tien Wah Press.

4   5   6   7   8   9   10

Library of Congress Cataloging-in-Publication Data
Maestro, Betsy.
The new Americans: Colonial times, 1620–1689/ by Betsy and Giulio Maestro.
p. cm.
Includes index.
Summary: Traces the competition among the American Indians, French, English, Spanish, and Dutch
for land, furs, timber, and other resources of North America.
ISBN 0-688-13448-3 (trade)—ISBN 0-688-13449-1 (library)
1. United States—History—Colonial period, ca. 1600–1775—Juvenile literature.   2. Canada—
History—To 1763 (New France)—Juvenile literature.   [1. United States—History—Colonial period, ca.
1600–1775.   2. Canada—History—To 1763 (New France).]   I. Maestro, Giulio.   II.Title.
E191.M34   1998   970.02—dc20   95-19636   CIP AC

6019297355

N THE HUNDRED YEARS FOLLOWING THE VOYAGES OF Christopher Columbus, many other European explorers sailed across the Atlantic Ocean to reach the New World. At first they came in search of new trade routes to the Far East. Then, as the riches of the Americas were discovered, the explorers were followed by conquerors and, later, by settlers. Spain, with her strong naval fleet, ruled the seas, and by 1600 her treasury was filled with gold and silver stolen from the people of South America and Mexico. The Spanish left the colder, seemingly worthless region of North America to the other countries of Europe whose ships were asail on the oceans of the world.

In South America, the Spanish seized silver mines at Potosí. They used Indian slave labor to remove more than eighteen thousand tons of silver ore from the mountain. The ore was crushed by mechanical hammers powered by a waterwheel, then mixed with mercury to extract the silver used to mint coins.

In the 1500s, Portuguese fishermen processed their catch at their seasonal settlement near Cape Breton, Nova Scotia.

The other European countries eagerly joined in the search for trade and treasure. However, the riches they found were not those they first sought. Although North America had great wealth, it wasn't in gold or silver. The true treasure of the north was in its other natural resources—an abundance of fish, furs, and lumber, all in great demand in Europe.

Early in the 1600s, French explorers established fur-trading posts in the wooded wilderness along the St. Lawrence River. To the south, the Dutch sailed up the Hudson River, and the English searched the Virginia coast for a site on which to build a permanent colony. European fishermen, already reaping harvests off Newfoundland, began to fish the waters of what would soon be called New England.

Soon after their arrival in Canada, the French began trading with Native Americans. The Indians brought furs to exchange for tools and cloth.

To the Europeans, North America at first seemed to be a vast and empty wilderness with plenty of land to take as they wished. However, they soon discovered that the continent was already occupied. About three hundred thousand Americans, called Indians by the Europeans, lived in the northeastern section of what is now the United States and Canada. More than one million Indians—possibly many more—peopled the continent north of Mexico. Their ancestors had arrived in the "New World" thousands of years before.

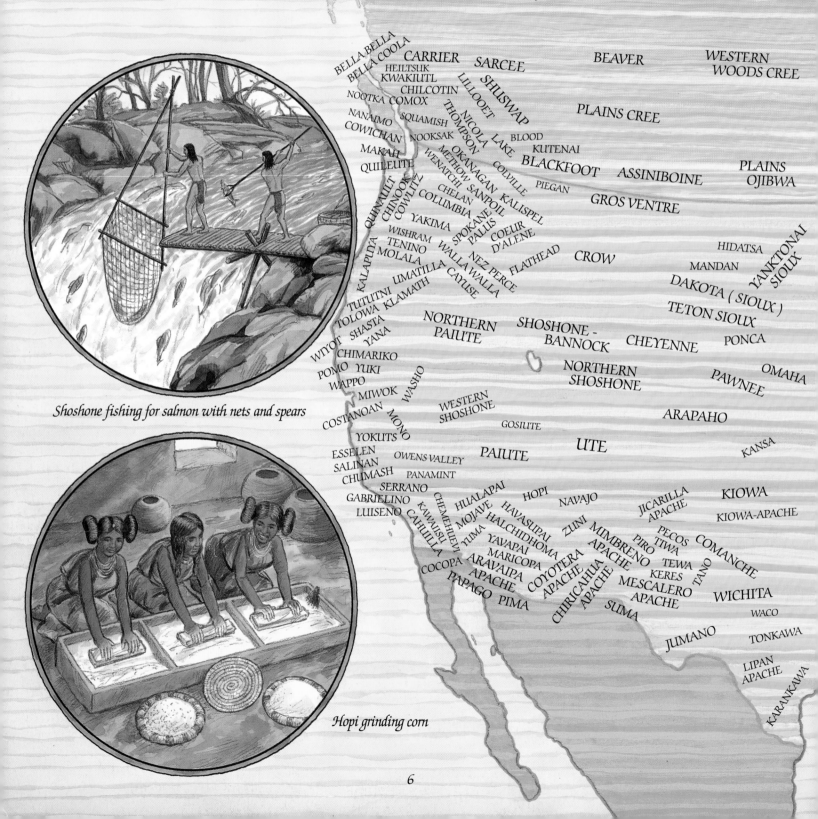

Shoshone fishing for salmon with nets and spears

Hopi grinding corn

BELLA BELLA
BELLA COOLA
CARRIER
SARCEE
BEAVER
WESTERN WOODS CREE
HEILTSUK
KWAKIUTL
CHILCOTIN
SHUSWAP
NOOTKA COMOX
LILLOOET
PLAINS CREE
NANAIMO SQUAMISH
NICOLA
THOMPSON
LAKE
BLOOD
KUTENAI
COWICHAN NOOKSAK
OKANAGAN KALISPEL
COLVILLE
BLACKFOOT
ASSINIBOINE
PLAINS OJIBWA
MAKAH
METHOW SANPOIL
PIEGAN
QUILEUTE
WENATCHI
GROS VENTRE
QUINAULT
CHINOOK
CHELAN
COLUMBIA
COWLITZ
YAKIMA
SPOKANE
PALUS
COEUR D'ALENE
HIDATSA
KALAPUYA
WISHRAM
NEZ PERCE
MANDAN
YANKTONAI SIOUX
TENINO
WALLA WALLA
FLATHEAD
CROW
MOLALA
UMATILLA
CAYUSE
DAKOTA (SIOUX)
TUTUTNI
TENINO
KLAMATH
NORTHERN
PAIUTE
SHOSHONE-
BANNOCK
TETON SIOUX
TOLOWA SHASTA
YANA
CHEYENNE
PONCA
WIYOT
CHIMARIKO
NORTHERN
SHOSHONE
OMAHA
POMO YUKI
WAPPO
WASHO
PAWNEE
MIWOK
WESTERN
SHOSHONE
COSTANOAN
MONO
ARAPAHO
YOKUTS
GOSIUTE
ESSELEN
UTE
KANSA
SALINAN
OWENS VALLEY
PAIUTE
CHUMASH
PANAMINT
SERRANO
KIOWA
GABRIELINO
HUALAPAI
HOPI
NAVAJO
JICARILLA APACHE
LUISENO
CHEMEHUEVI
MOJAVE
HAVASUPAI
KIOWA-APACHE
CAHUILLA
KAWAIISU
YUMA
HALCHIDHOMA
ZUNI
MIMBRENO
PECOS
TIWA
COMANCHE
YAVAPAI
MARICOPA
COYOTERA
APACHE
PIRO
TEWA
COCOPA ARAVAIPA
APACHE
CHIRICAHUA
APACHE
KERES
TANO
PAPAGO PIMA
MESCALERO
APACHE
WICHITA
SUMA
WACO
JUMANO
TONKAWA
LIPAN
APACHE
KARANKAWA

The Indians felt themselves to be the rightful caretakers of the lands they lived on. They had hunted, planted, and fished in North America long before the first European ships appeared on the horizon. The arrival of the European traders and settlers led to great changes in the lives of Native Americans. In the long struggle for land, trade, and food, the French, English, Dutch, and Spanish formed complex relationships with the Indians—relationships that would shape the future of the North American continent.

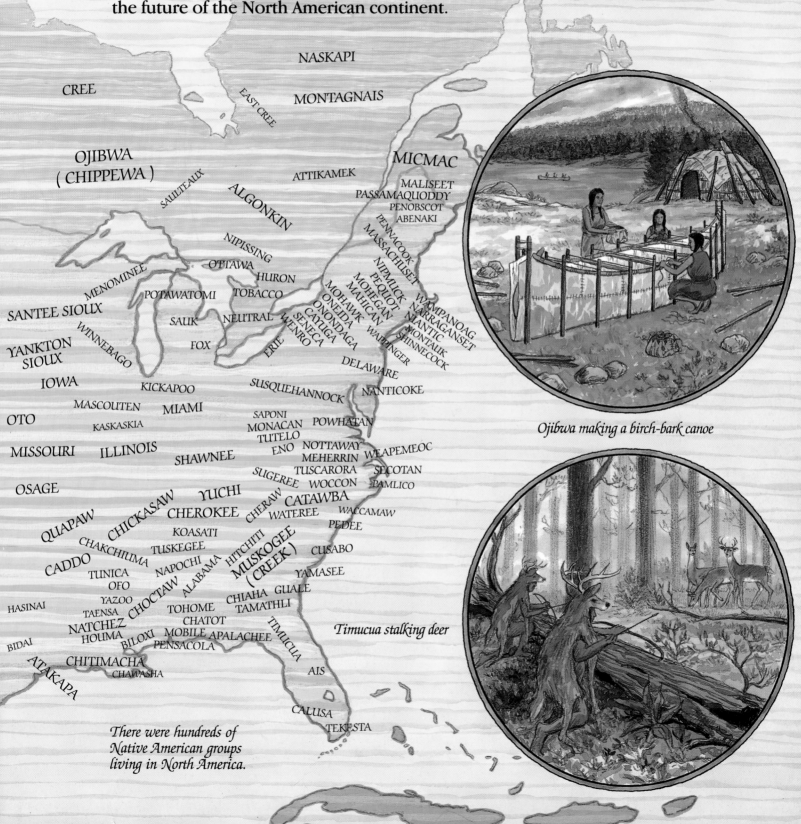

NASKAPI

CREE

MONTAGNAIS

EAST CREE

OJIBWA
(CHIPPEWA)

MICMAC

ATTIKAMEK

SAULTEAUX

ALGONKIN

MALISEET
PASSAMAQUODDY
PENOBSCOT
ABENAKI

NIPISSING

PENNACOOK
MASSACHUSET
NIPMUCK
PEQUOT
MOHEGAN
MAHICAN
MOHAWK
ONEIDA
ONONDAGA
CAYUGA
SENECA
WENRO
WAPPINGER
SHINNECOCK

WAMPANOAG
NARRAGANSET
NIANTIC
MONTAUK

OTTAWA

HURON

TOBACCO

MENOMINEE

POTAWATOMI

SAUK

NEUTRAL

ERIE

DELAWARE

SANTEE SIOUX

WINNEBAGO

FOX

YANKTON
SIOUX

SUSQUEHANNOCK

NANTICOKE

IOWA

KICKAPOO

MASCOUTEN

MIAMI

SAPONI
MONACAN
TUTELO

POWHATAN

OTO

KASKASKIA

ENO

NOTTAWAY
MEHERRIN
TUSCARORA

WEAPEMEOC

MISSOURI

ILLINOIS

SHAWNEE

SECOTAN

SUGEREE

WOCCON

PAMLICO

OSAGE

YUCHI

CHEROKEE

CHERAW

CATAWBA

WATEREE

WACCAMAW

QUAPAW

CHICKASAW

KOASATI

PEDEE

CHAKCHIUMA

TUSKEGEE

CADDO

NAPOCHI

HITCHITI

MUSKOGEE
(CREEK)

CUSABO

TUNICA

ALABAMA

OFO

CHOCTAW

YAMASEE

HASINAI

YAZOO

TOHOME

CHIAHA

GUALE

TAENSA

CHATOT

TAMATHLI

NATCHEZ

HOUMA

BILOXI

MOBILE

APALACHEE

TIMUCUA

BIDAI

PENSACOLA

CHITIMACHA

CHAWASHA

AIS

ATAKAPA

CALUSA

TEKESTA

Ojibwa making a birch-bark canoe

Timucua stalking deer

There were hundreds of Native American groups living in North America.

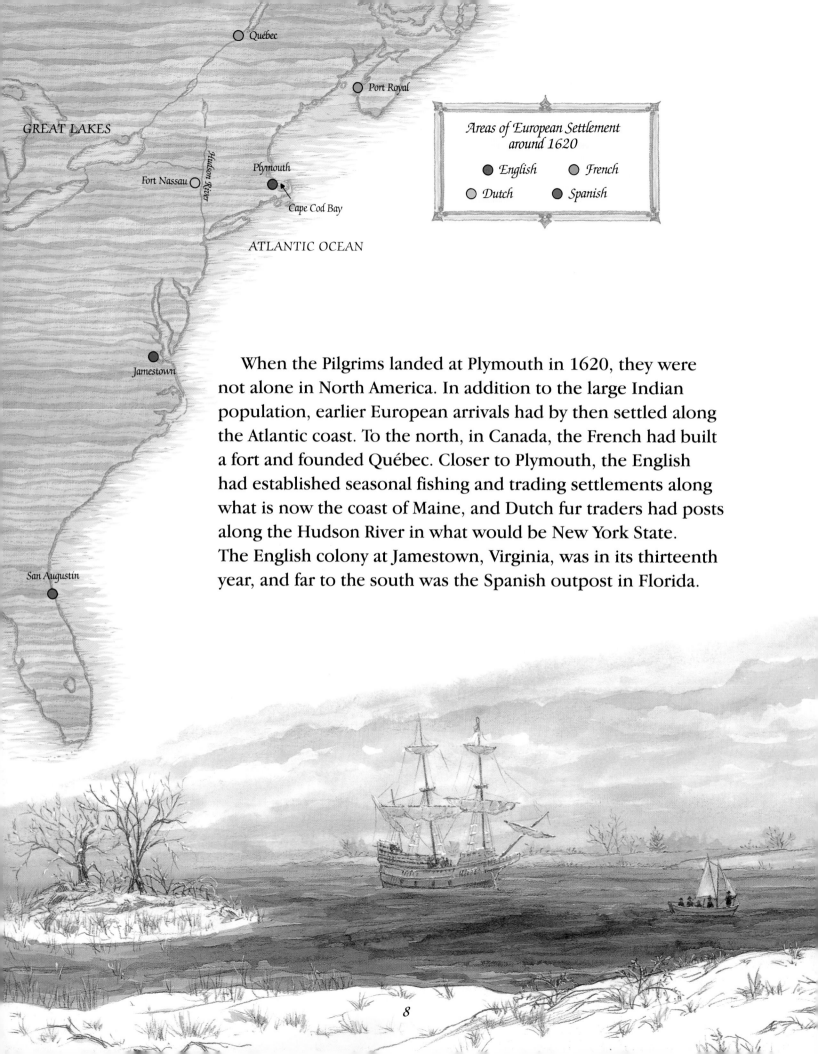

Québec

Port Royal

GREAT LAKES

Fort Nassau

Plymouth

Cape Cod Bay

*Areas of European Settlement
around 1620*

● *English*   ● *French*
○ *Dutch*   ● *Spanish*

ATLANTIC OCEAN

Jamestown

San Augustín

When the Pilgrims landed at Plymouth in 1620, they were not alone in North America. In addition to the large Indian population, earlier European arrivals had by then settled along the Atlantic coast. To the north, in Canada, the French had built a fort and founded Québec. Closer to Plymouth, the English had established seasonal fishing and trading settlements along what is now the coast of Maine, and Dutch fur traders had posts along the Hudson River in what would be New York State. The English colony at Jamestown, Virginia, was in its thirteenth year, and far to the south was the Spanish outpost in Florida.

The Pilgrims and the other settlers aboard the *Mayflower* had intended to join the Virginia colonists. Instead, their captain held to a westward course, and in November he brought them into Cape Cod Bay. Even before their first landing to find food and explore, the voyagers wrote and signed a set of laws for the new colony. This agreement, called the Mayflower Compact, would help the settlers stick together in the hard times ahead.

Over the freezing winter, while simple wooden houses were built on the site they had chosen at Plymouth, many of the settlers continued to live aboard the *Mayflower.* By March, when the weather had warmed and some houses were ready, more than half of the one hundred and two colonists had died of fever and illness.

The Mayflower Compact was signed by the male passengers aboard the ship to protect the rights and safety of all the colonists.

The Pilgrims found their chosen site well prepared for human settlement. Although they did not know it, the land had been cleared by Indians who had lived there not long before. Most of those natives had died of smallpox, measles, and pneumonia brought by European fishermen and explorers, and the survivors had joined other nearby tribes.

Although the Pilgrims saw no Indians during the first few months, the local tribes were well aware of their arrival. In March, they began to appear and introduce themselves. By incredible luck, these settlers from England had landed at a place the Indians called Patuxet, where not just one but two Indians were able to speak English, which they had learned from earlier contacts.

Squanto showed the Pilgrims how to fertilize their corn by placing dried fish in the ground with the seeds.

Squanto, who had been kidnapped and taken to Europe years before, spoke the most English. He came to live with the Pilgrims and showed them how to plant corn, fish with nets, and hunt deer. The relationship that grew between the Pilgrims and their neighbors, the Wampanoags, was friendly and cooperative. The new settlers signed a peace treaty with Massasoit, the leader of all the area tribes.

By the following fall, when the feast we call Thanksgiving first took place, the Pilgrims had settled into their new lives. They had plenty to eat, comfortable houses, and nothing to fear from their new neighbors. Unfortunately, the peace and serenity would not last long.

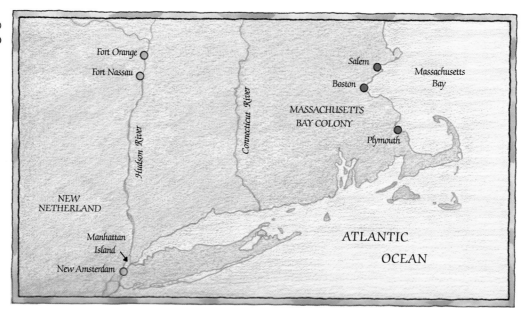

Some Dutch ○
and English ●
Settlements
around 1630

Fort Orange ●

Fort Nassau ●

Salem ●

Boston ●

Massachusetts Bay

Hudson River

Connecticut River

MASSACHUSETTS BAY COLONY

Plymouth ●

NEW NETHERLAND

Manhattan Island →

New Amsterdam ○

ATLANTIC

OCEAN

Even before the English settlers arrived at Plymouth, other newcomers landed along the Hudson River. The Dutch began to come to America after the voyages of Henry Hudson. As early as 1612, they were trading with Indians on Manhattan Island, at the mouth of the Hudson. Two years later, they built Fort Nassau near where the city of Albany, New York, now stands. As the Pilgrims settled into their lives at Plymouth, the Dutch colony of New Netherland was coming to life in the Hudson Valley.

New Amsterdam in the 1600s

In 1626, Dutch settlers bought Manhattan Island from local Indians.

The Dutch settlement called New Amsterdam was constructed at the tip of Manhattan Island, in the spring of 1625. The following year, Governor Peter Minuit arrived, bringing more colonists. He is said to have arranged a now famous swap with local Indians: For trade goods with a value of about sixty Dutch guilders (equal to something like twenty-four dollars), he received all of Manhattan Island. This wooded island would later become part of the city of New York. In the following years, spurred on by the trading interests of the Dutch West India Company, thousands of Dutch settlers arrived in the Hudson Valley and New Amsterdam. A small group of traders ventured as far south as Delaware Bay.

Unlike the Dutch, who had come to the New World to trade, the Pilgrims had come in search of religious freedom. Most people in England were Protestants and belonged to the Church of England. The practice of other religions was forbidden, so Catholics and Protestants with different ideas were forced to worship in secret. The Pilgrims were Separatists—people who wished to break away, or separate, from the Church of England in order to worship in their own way.

Other Protestants, called Puritans, wanted to remain within the Church of England to bring about change. They believed that the church needed to be cleansed, or purified, by simplifying its rituals. They had little hope of bringing about these changes in England. So, like the Pilgrims, they too looked to America.

The Puritans were given a royal charter, an agreement with the king of England, that granted them land for the colony they would call Massachusetts Bay. A great migration of Puritans began in 1630, and the towns and cities they founded, including Boston and Salem, soon thrived along the Massachusetts coast.

John Winthrop, who led Puritans to America in 1630, served as the first governor of the Massachusetts Bay Colony.

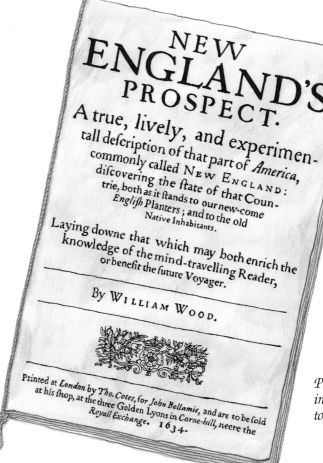

Pamphlets were printed in England to attract more settlers to Massachusetts.

*New Connecticut colonists
hear their first Sunday sermon.*

Over the next few years, more than ten thousand Puritans arrived in the Massachusetts Bay Colony. They began to spread inland, away from Boston and the coast, to settle frontier towns in western Massachusetts. Some sailed up the Connecticut River to settle the valley near Hartford, where the Dutch had earlier built a fort. Others founded settlements along the Connecticut shore to the south, and in coastal Maine and New Hampshire to the north.

Although the Puritans had come to America to find religious freedom, they did not allow for it in their own colony. Their leaders were strict Puritans who believed that there was only one way to worship God—their way. Those who thought that the church should be separate from the government, or that people should be able to pray as they wished, were not allowed to speak out. In fact, they were not welcome in the colony at all.

Whole families were punished and forced to leave the Massachusetts Bay Colony.

After her trial, Anne Hutchinson was banished from Massachusetts. She led a group of followers to Rhode Island in 1638.

Many dissenters left Massachusetts Bay to begin settlements elsewhere. Some, like Roger Williams and Anne Hutchinson, were persecuted and punished for speaking out about religious freedom. In 1635, Williams, a minister in Salem, fled the colony on foot, through the winter snow, to avoid arrest. Chief Massasoit, a friend from his days in Plymouth, sheltered him in an Indian village near Narragansett Bay until spring. The next year, Roger Williams founded Providence, which became the capital of a new colony, Rhode Island. Religious freedom was offered to all who settled there.

The Wampanoags offered Roger Williams a home for the winter.

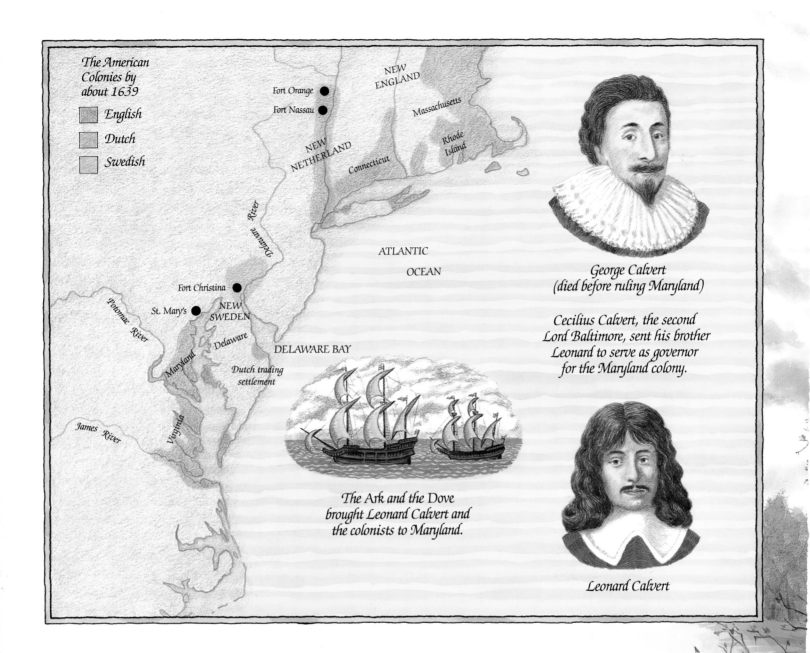

The American Colonies by about 1639

English
Dutch
Swedish

NEW ENGLAND

Fort Orange
Fort Nassau

Massachusetts

NEW NETHERLAND

Connecticut

Rhode Island

Delaware River

ATLANTIC OCEAN

Fort Christina
St. Mary's
NEW SWEDEN

Potomac River

Maryland

Delaware

DELAWARE BAY

Dutch trading settlement

James River

Virginia

George Calvert
(died before ruling Maryland)

Cecilius Calvert, the second Lord Baltimore, sent his brother Leonard to serve as governor for the Maryland colony.

The Ark and the Dove brought Leonard Calvert and the colonists to Maryland.

Leonard Calvert

A few years earlier, the English king had granted land for another American colony to George Calvert, a Catholic, whose title was Lord Baltimore. In 1634, two hundred English settlers landed along the Potomac River. There they founded Maryland, along the Atlantic coast between the colonies in Massachusetts and Virginia.

Although Maryland was founded as a haven for Catholics, half of the first group of settlers were Protestants. As the colony grew, so did its Protestant population, and within a short time, they were in the majority. Protestants were resentful of the power held by the Calverts and other wealthy Catholics, and fighting broke out. Civil war between these two religious groups marred the early years of the Maryland colony.

Not far away, Fort Christina, the first settlement of New Sweden, was founded in 1638. A company of Swedish merchants encouraged emigration to America. They hired Peter Minuit to guide the first Swedish settlers across the Atlantic to the small colony named for the Swedish queen.

Over the years, both Swedes and Finns arrived in the colony that would soon be called Delaware. These settlers brought the Lutheran religion and the log cabin to America. These dwellings were strong and durable, as well as easy to build and heat. Within a short time, log cabins were common in the wilderness and on the American frontier.

Settlers prepared a tree for log cabin construction by peeling the bark around the base, causing the tree to dry out and die.

Settlers had no warning of surprise Indian attacks.

As the number of white settlers increased, the Indians were pushed into smaller and smaller areas. Many tribes in Connecticut and Massachusetts became angry and resentful. The Pequots in eastern Connecticut were among the first to feel hemmed in, with the Dutch to their south and west and the English to their north and east. For more than ten years, there had been relative peace in the colonies, but in 1636, after the Pequots were blamed for the deaths of some white traders, fighting broke out between settlers and Indians.

Both sides led raids on villages and settlements, brutally killing innocent people. New England colonists united and formed an army, aided by Narraganset, Niantic, and Mohegan Indians, who were enemies of the Pequots. In 1637, these forces attacked a stockaded Pequot village and burned it to the ground. More than six hundred Pequot men, women, and children were killed, and the survivors were sold as slaves. The Pequot War soon ended, but the fighting was far from over.

Captain John Mason led the attack on a Pequot village, even though it held mostly women and children.

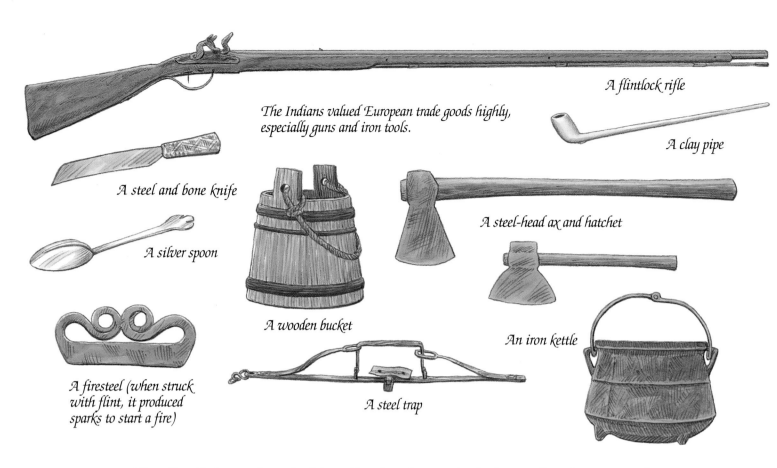

A flintlock rifle

The Indians valued European trade goods highly, especially guns and iron tools.

A clay pipe

A steel and bone knife

A steel-head ax and hatchet

A silver spoon

A wooden bucket

An iron kettle

A firesteel (when struck with flint, it produced sparks to start a fire)

A steel trap

The English settlers in New England worried about the dangers of Indian raids. But they also worried about the French and the Dutch, who were looking for ways to expand their trading territory. While the English settlers thought of America mainly as a place to live, the Dutch and the French were much more interested in the very profitable fur trade. Beaver pelts were in great demand in Europe, where they were used to make popular felt hats.

The Iroquois lived in large family groups in longhouses—communal dwellings made of wooden frames and often covered in elm bark.

The fine hair shaved from beaver pelts was used to make felt. From the 1600s to the 1800s, Indian traders could hardly keep up with the demand for furs.

The European fur trade depended almost totally on the Indians for supply. The Dutch had established a trading relationship with the Iroquois, a powerful group of tribes united by language and government. Five of the Iroquois nations—the Mohawk, Oneida, Onondaga, Cayuga, and Seneca— had joined in a league that brought them strength, protection, and peaceful relations with one another.

The Dutch and the Iroquois needed each other. The Dutch colony depended on Indian trade for its income, and the Iroquois had come to rely on European goods they received in exchange for furs. The Iroquois particularly needed and wanted guns and ammunition, for they were preparing to challenge their rivals and enemies to the north—the Hurons and their French protectors.

In New France, which is now part of Canada, the Hurons and the French controlled most of the North American fur trade. The Hurons were an Iroquoian tribe but not a member of the Iroquois League. They had allied themselves with both the French and the Algonquian tribes for protection and cooperation in the fur trade. Many of the Indian tribes living in the northeast woodlands and Great Lakes areas were Algonquians. These tribes spoke variations of the same language, had many common customs, and had often been victims of the aggressive Iroquois.

Ojibwa men and women crafted birch-bark canoes at their encampments. These Algonquian boats were light and fast—ideal for both calm lakes and river rapids.

The Hurons were the middlemen. They traded their produce for furs from Algonquian tribes farther inland. Then they transported the furs eastward to the French at Québec or Montréal, to be exchanged for cloth, knives, metal pots, and beads. Every spring, Huron canoes arrived in the French settlements loaded with furs from the interior.

Huron and French traders exchange goods at Montréal.

Of all the European intruders in the Indian world, it was the French who came to know the native people best. Beginning with Samuel de Champlain, the founder of Québec, Frenchmen did not always assume that European ideas and customs were superior. They lived with, listened to, and learned from their Indian trading partners, with whom they shared trust, loyalty, and often friendship.

Frenchmen called *voyageurs* (travelers) and *coureurs de bois* (runners of the woods) earned their livings working in the fur trade. These men lived in the wilderness, often with the Indians. They came to know Indian languages and lifeways. There was respect and appreciation on both sides. In the years ahead, these independent adventurers would be forced to find new suppliers of fur and new middlemen for the trade. The Iroquois were on the warpath, and the Huron would soon be destroyed.

The Ottawa, as well as other Indians, found
European iron kettles and wooden kegs useful for
making maple syrup and sugar.

27

The Iroquois had greatly depleted the fur supply close to their homelands and needed a larger share of the Canadian fur trade in order to survive. But they also wanted revenge. They had not forgotten how the French had helped the Hurons to defeat them years before. Intense rivalry grew among the many tribes that were involved in the fur trade. The Iroquois longed to end French-Huron control.

Despite their great importance in the fur trade, the Huron nation was not strong. Over the years, disease brought by the French and disagreement over the adoption of French religion and culture had weakened the Hurons.

Hurons often visited the Jesuit mission settlement of Ste. Marie at Georgian Bay in Canada.

The Beaver Wars began when the Iroquois attacked Huron settlements in 1649. The Hurons were unable to defend themselves against the strength of the massive Iroquois attack, and French settlers were too few to aid their embattled friends.

The wars raged on and off for many years, with the Iroquois League bringing death and destruction to tribes from the Hudson Valley to the Great Lakes. Tobaccos and Neutrals, Eries and Ottawas, Illinois and Miamis all fell victim to their terrible power. Only the arrival of French troops in 1667 ended the fighting.

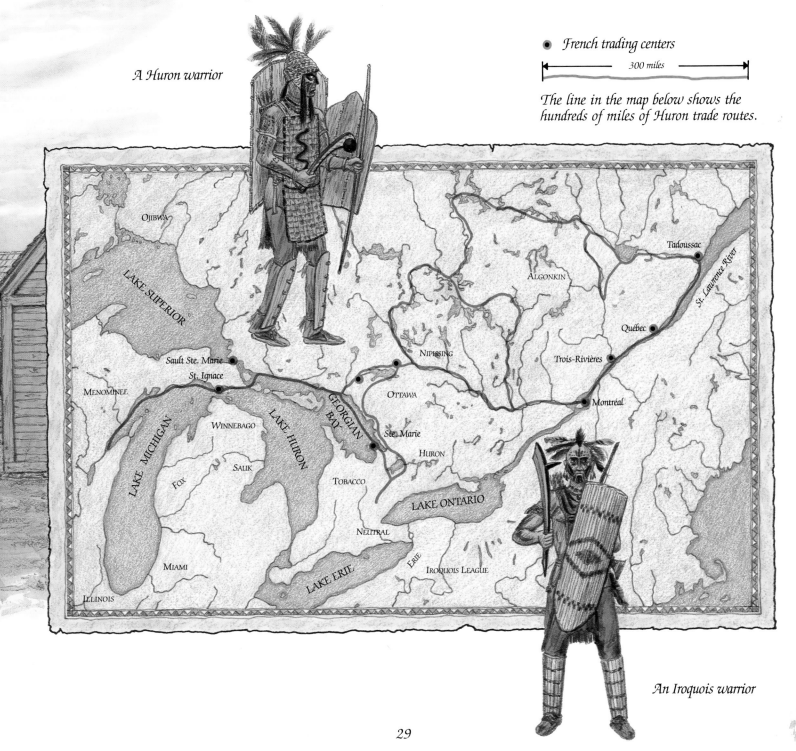

A Huron warrior

● *French trading centers*

|←——— *300 miles* ———→|

The line in the map below shows the hundreds of miles of Huron trade routes.

An Iroquois warrior

Jesuit priests baptized many Indians as converts to the Catholic faith.

From the beginning of the French presence in North America, French priests called Jesuits had accompanied traders and explorers as they moved inland. Jesuits soon moved out on their own to remote Indian villages, in the hopes of converting native people to the Catholic faith. These priest-explorers slowly wandered west along Indian trails to the Great Lakes. Their travels expanded French knowledge of this region and of the Indians who lived there. Like the *voyageurs* and *coureurs de bois,* the Jesuits explored and mapped the interior, expanding the borders of New France as they went.

The Beaver Wars interrupted exploration and slowed the fur trade. *Coureurs de bois* filled in for the embattled Huron to keep the flow of furs moving east. The French began to look farther west for new links to the fur supply.

Two French woodsmen, Pierre Radisson and Médard Chouart, Sieur de Groseilliers, traveled west to Lake Superior in 1659. They were looking for a way to shorten the long overland journey from the Great Lakes to Québec and Montréal. They had the idea of transporting the furs north instead—to Hudson Bay—and then by ship to France. When French officials in Québec showed no enthusiasm, the English became interested in the plan. In 1668, Groseilliers sailed to Hudson Bay and returned to England with a cargo of furs. Two years later, the Hudson Bay Trading Company was established. Soon the Cree were bringing their furs to the English forts along Hudson Bay. The French were not pleased by this unwelcome competition.

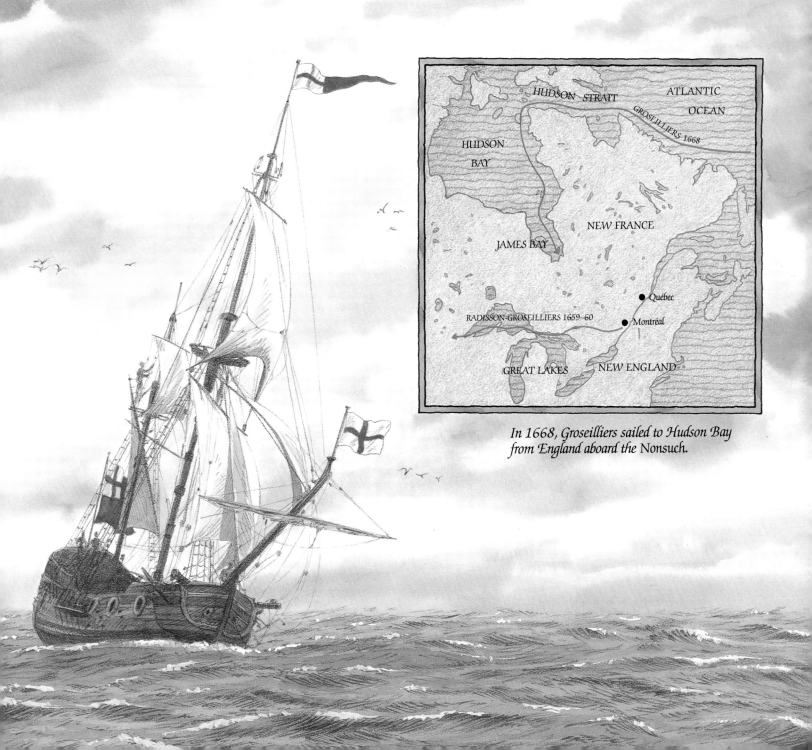

In 1668, Groseilliers sailed to Hudson Bay from England aboard the Nonsuch.

While the French and the Dutch had been protecting and expanding their trading empires, the English had been busy bringing more settlers to America. Many more colonists had arrived from England than had come from either France or the Netherlands, and the newcomers needed more and more land. Now it was the French and the Dutch who worried about English expansion—with good reason.

In 1664, the English captured New Amsterdam from the Dutch without firing a single shot. The Dutch, who were greatly outnumbered, quickly surrendered at the sight of English ships in the harbor. New Amsterdam became New York.

Peter Stuyvesant was enraged by the English demand to surrender New Amsterdam, but he was not equipped to defend it.

New Amsterdam in 1664

Soon England controlled all of New Netherland—more than thirty settlements, including a huge tract of land made up of what is now most of New York, New Jersey, Pennsylvania, and Delaware (which the Dutch had captured from Sweden). By 1670, the population in the English colonies had grown to over one hundred thousand, and the English controlled all of the Atlantic coast from Maine to Spanish Florida.

They had gained the use of two broad, navigable rivers—the Hudson and the Delaware—and inherited the Dutch trading alliance with the Iroquois. This partnership would prove to be very important to the English. The Iroquois controlled vast trade and territory, and they shared a common enemy with the English—the French. With the Iroquois as allies, the English would be better able to challenge the French for land and trade.

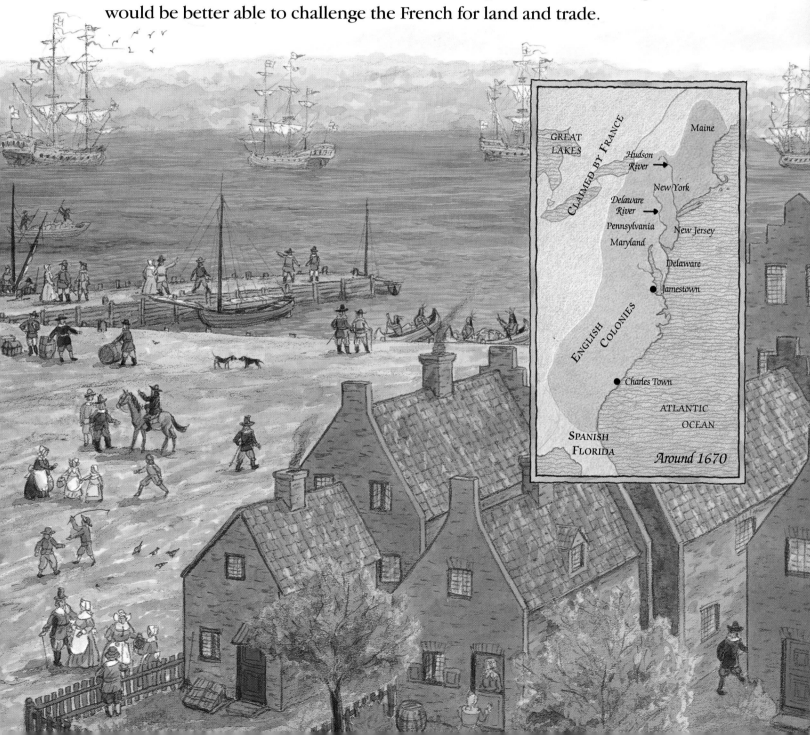

GREAT LAKES

CLAIMED BY FRANCE

Maine

Hudson River →

New York

Delaware River →

Pennsylvania

New Jersey

Maryland

Delaware

● Jamestown

ENGLISH COLONIES

● Charles Town

ATLANTIC OCEAN

SPANISH FLORIDA

Around 1670

But there were other problems to deal with first. Despite friendly relations with the Iroquois, the English faced a growing threat of Algonquian uprisings in New England and Virginia, where there were frequent disputes over land and hunting rights. Many white settlers were unfair in their dealings with the Indians, tricking or cheating them out of what had been promised. In Plymouth and Massachusetts Bay, the colonists demanded more and more land, and insisted that the Indians follow English laws and pay English taxes. The Indians rebelled.

Indians used fire arrows to ignite the colonists' wooden houses.

Metacom, called King Philip by the English, was the son of Massasoit and had become leader of the Wampanoags. In 1675, he put together an alliance of tribes in an effort to reclaim their homelands. Narragansetts, Nipmucs, and others joined King Philip's war against the settlers. But the Mohegans, Niantics, Massachusets, and others fought alongside the colonial militia. Within a year, Metacom was killed, and the rebellion was put down. The war left thousands dead, a number of towns destroyed, and many tribes all but wiped out. With Indian strength and resistance gone, colonists felt free to move wherever they pleased. Soon there would be few Indians left in New England.

The City Tavern, originally opened by the Dutch in 1642, became New York's first City Hall.

Colonial shipyards employed thousands of workers.

In 1657, Boston's Town House held the offices of the General Court, with an open marketplace underneath.

In spite of Indian wars and religious intolerance, the English colonies thrived. In the north, the city of Boston was a bustling port—home to cod fishing and shipbuilding. New England fishermen put out to sea on a fleet of more than five hundred ships.

New York City, another busy seaport, had a large population that included people from about twenty different countries. Compared to Puritan Boston, New York City was a place of great diversity and tolerance—a place where Protestants, Catholics, Quakers, Lutherans, and Jews all worshiped freely. The first Jewish settlers had arrived in 1654, fleeing religious persecution in Spain.

New England streams provided the waterpower for sawmills.

As the population in the English colonies grew, so did trade and industry. The colonists became more independent, making many products themselves instead of relying on England for all their supplies. Earlier, in 1643, the first textile mill had opened in Massachusetts, and a few years later, furniture making began in the Connecticut Valley.

Travel within the colonies was difficult and extremely slow. Roads were rough and unpaved, and when mail service between Boston and New York began in 1673, the one-way trip on horseback took about three weeks.

Braving the winter weather, the mail carrier announced his arrival with a post horn.

William Penn

A Pennsylvania farm

The English colonies were also growing in number. In 1682, William Penn, an English Quaker, led a group of settlers to the colony he named Pennsylvania. Penn promised democratic government and religious freedom for all. Members of religious groups who had been persecuted elsewhere were invited to come to Pennsylvania. Quakers settled in the fertile farmlands, and German Mennonites founded a community outside the new city of Philadelphia.

In the south, settlements in the Carolinas had been established to give Virginia more protection from the Indians and the Spanish. As early as 1653, colonists from Virginia moved into what would later be North Carolina.

The city of Charleston, South Carolina, founded as Charles Town in 1670, would soon become a thriving port. Rice cultivation began in the Carolina wetlands, and tobacco from plantations in Virginia and Maryland was shipped regularly across the Atlantic. The sale of these crops brought in needed trade goods, as well as coins and paper currency—always in short supply, as Britain did not allow the colonists to make their own money.

From its very beginning in Jamestown, the southern plantation system depended on the labor of slaves taken by force from Africa. The first slaves had come to Virginia in 1619 on a Dutch ship, and within a short time, thousands were brought to America. Although many colonists were against slavery, rich merchants and landowners in the north, as well as the plantation owners in the south, depended on the slave trade for their livelihood. So slavery survived, despite the human misery it caused.

Heavy barrels of tobacco were rolled onto ships on the James River in Virginia.

Slavery became part of colonial life, because cheap labor meant higher profits when crops were sold in England. Many colonists were willing to overlook the evils of slavery.

England was happy that its colonies in America were doing so well. However, the English government didn't want the colonies to forget that they were founded to benefit their mother country and not themselves. England wanted America's valuable trade all for itself. So between 1650 and 1696, the British Parliament passed a series of laws called the Navigation Acts to restrict American trade. These acts made it clear that all American products had to be shipped to England on English ships. The colonies were not free to trade with other countries, and American ships were not free to sail where they pleased. The colonists were furious about these restrictions, and when England wasn't looking, they began to disobey them.

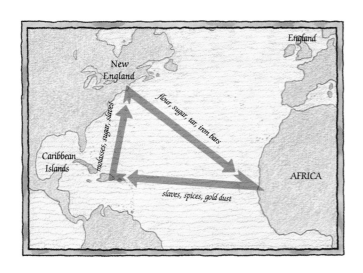

Toward the end of the 1600s, New England shipowners began to defy the Navigation Acts by making use of this triangular trade route: Goods were shipped to Africa and traded for slaves. Slaves were sold in the West Indies in exchange for sugar and molasses, which the colonists took home and used to make rum.

It wasn't hard for the American colonists to defy English law. England had little time to keep a close eye on America. With so many interests to protect around the world, British officials couldn't possibly oversee them all. So they sent royal governors to manage colonial affairs. But British interference was met with hostility and anger, and the colonial governors were often extremely unpopular. Many colonists had begun to think of themselves not as English citizens, but as Americans.

King James II wanted to tighten English control over the colonies.

In 1686, Sir Edmund Andros was appointed by the king to govern New England. He was ordered to take back the charters, or permits, granted to the colonies by England.

The Connecticut colonists hid their charter in a hollow oak tree for fourteen years. By the end of that period, Andros had been called back to England.

Marquette and Joliet traveled south, down the Mississippi, to the mouth of the Arkansas River.

As England expanded her territory in North America, the French moved to do the same. Though the French population in America had barely grown over the years, the borders of New France had continually expanded as explorers pushed south and west. Traveling Jesuit priests had heard tales of a great river with an Indian name that sounded like "Michissipi." Rivers were the highways of the wilderness—the highways the French needed to take them west to the Pacific Ocean. Some years before, in 1673, fur trader Louis Joliet and Father Jacques Marquette had led a small expedition down this great river. They traveled many hundreds of miles before learning that the Mississippi did not lead west, as they had hoped, but flowed south instead, to the Gulf of Mexico and Spanish territory.

Joliet

Marquette

La Salle

In 1681, René-Robert Cavelier, Sieur de La Salle, headed another expedition down the Mississippi. About fifty Frenchmen and Indians followed the route of Joliet and Marquette and then continued south to the mouth of this mighty river. In April 1682, La Salle claimed the entire Mississippi River and its valley for France. New France now controlled the center of North America from the Great Lakes to the Gulf of Mexico. The French soon built trading posts and forts along the Mississippi and in the vast area that the French named Louisiana, after their king, Louis XIV.

La Salle's party of twenty-three Frenchmen was accompanied by twenty-eight Indian men and women and three Indian children.

Louisiana was not far away from the Spanish missions and forts in Florida, which the Spanish had occupied since they founded San Augustín in 1565. When the English ventured south from the Carolinas, and the roving French reached the Gulf of Mexico, Spain readied to defend the territory it had seized from the Indians years before.

The southeast was not the only area of conflict. As the French moved south from Canada and the English moved inland toward the Mississippi River, traders, explorers, and settlers pushed their way into the Ohio Valley. As they claimed territory for themselves and for their countries, bitter rivalries and bloody conflicts erupted between the French and the English.

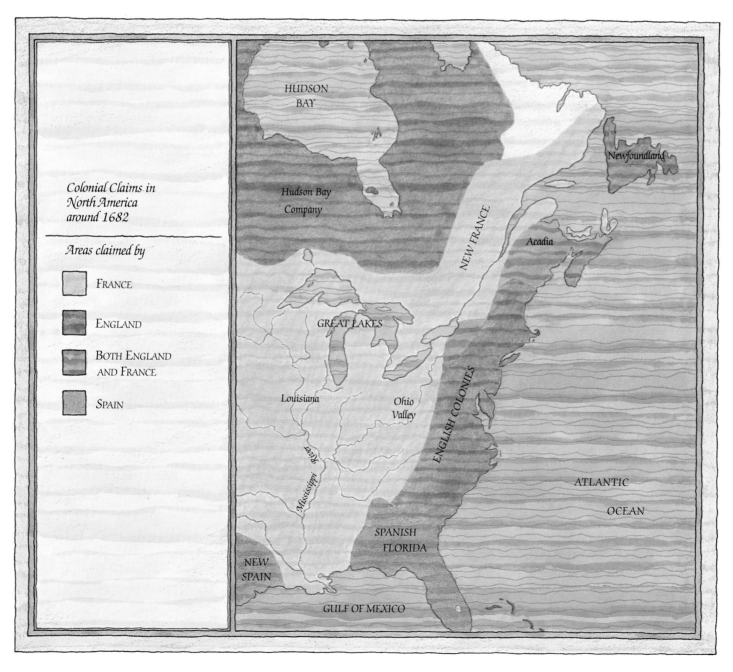

Colonial Claims in North America around 1682

Areas claimed by

FRANCE

ENGLAND

BOTH ENGLAND AND FRANCE

SPAIN

HUDSON BAY

Newfoundland

Hudson Bay Company

NEW FRANCE

Acadia

GREAT LAKES

Louisiana

Ohio Valley

ENGLISH COLONIES

Mississippi River

ATLANTIC

OCEAN

SPANISH FLORIDA

NEW SPAIN

GULF OF MEXICO

In the struggle to come, English soldiers with their red coats would be easy targets for the French and their Indian allies.

After thousands of years of Native American civilization, North America had been discovered by the Europeans. Kings and queens of Europe gave little thought to the fate of the thousands of Americans already living on the continent. They granted land as they pleased to traders and settlers, and they encouraged explorers to venture farther and farther into the interior of the huge continent.

But as large as North America was, it wasn't large enough to satisfy the greed of so many. The new Americans were unwilling to share land and trade with one another, just as they were unwilling to share land and trade with the first Americans. The encounters and challenges among the French, English, Spanish, and Indians grew increasingly hostile and violent. The victors would not be decided in a few days or months, but over the next seventy years. The struggle for a continent had begun, and the future of North America would be determined by its outcome.

Additional Information
More About Colonial America: 1620–1689

The first Indian to greet the Pilgrims was Samoset, an Abenaki from Maine who had learned English from European fishermen. At the time of the Pilgrims' arrival at Plymouth, he was a guest of the Wampanoag sachem Usamequin, also called Massasoit.

In 1639, the first post office in the colonies was operated by Richard Fairbanks out of his home in Boston, Massachusetts. He charged one penny for each letter. Years later, in the 1670s, colonial officials in New York City hired Indians to carry the mail to Albany during the winter months. They could be relied on to make it through the heavy snows when no one else could.

The first European settlement in Texas was founded at Yselta by Spaniards fleeing the Pueblo revolt in New Mexico. Because of hostilities with many local tribes, the settlement did not last. El Paso would later be built where Yselta once was.

Much of Jamestown, Virginia, was destroyed by fire in 1676, not in an Indian raid, but during a rebellion of settlers led by Nathaniel Bacon. The conflict occurred because many Virginians felt that the English colonial governor, Sir William Berkeley, was not protecting their lands from Indian raids. Jamestown was the capital of the Virginia colony until it was burned.

In 1652, the first colonial mint was established in Boston, Massachusetts. John Hull, a silversmith, was appointed master and asked to design a silver coin for the colony. Although it was against English colonial law for the colonists to make their own money, Hull minted a new coin called the pine tree shilling. The coin had a pine tree design stamped on one side.

In 1639, Margaret Brent, the first female lawyer in the colonies, spoke before the Maryland Assembly to ask for the right to vote. She was refused, even though she met the requirement of owning land. In 1655, Deborah Moody, a Dutch settler in New York, became the first woman to vote in a colonial assembly as a landowner.

Although Roger Williams is best known for founding the colony of Rhode Island, he was also an author. He compiled the first Native American dictionary. His book of Algonquian words was published in England in 1643.

In 1636, Harvard College was founded in Cambridge, Massachusetts. It was the first college in America. Young men who were schooled in Latin and the Greek classics were eligible for admission. In the early years, some students paid their tuition in livestock.

The first book of poetry in America was written by its first female poet. Anne Bradstreet had her first volume of poetry published in England in 1650. Another volume was published in Boston in 1678, after her death.

French Protestants, called Huguenots, fled religious persecution in France. They began to arrive in the American colonies in large numbers around 1685. Mostly middle-class merchants, they settled in New York, Rhode Island, Virginia, and the Carolinas. About five hundred Huguenots settled in Charles Town, South Carolina.

Toward the end of the 1630s, the European population in the English colonies was only about six thousand. By the end of the 1680s, the European population was more than two hundred thousand.

Exploration and Explorers: 1634–1685

From the beginning of the European presence in North America, there was great curiosity about what lay beyond the first areas of settlement. As the colonial population grew, there was more pressure to expand trade and extend borders. Many hardy, adventurous men—settlers, priests, traders, and land speculators—became explorers. As they moved north, west, and south, the borders between settlement and wilderness changed. Settlements and trading posts at the very edges of what was still wilderness formed the frontier, but the frontier was an ever-changing line. Frontier settlements were lonely and dangerous, always targets for Indian raids. Eventually, the westernmost borders met the Pacific Ocean, and the frontier ceased to exist.

Jean Nicolet became the first European to see Lake Michigan, in 1634.
John Lederer made three inland journeys in Virginia and the Carolinas in 1670.
Henry Woodward traveled through parts of the Carolinas and Georgia between 1670 and 1685.
Daniel Greysolon Dulhut explored parts of Minnesota and Lake Superior in 1679.
Father Louis Hennepin and *Henri de Tonty* accompanied La Salle on many of his expeditions. From 1678 to 1680, they explored the area around Niagara Falls, the Great Lakes, and the upper Mississippi River.
Eusebio Francisco Kino, a Spanish priest, made a series of explorations around and across the Gulf of California in the 1680s. In 1685, he reached the Pacific coast.

The Explorations of John Smith

Captain John Smith, a leader of Jamestown, led expeditions in Virginia in 1607. The next year, he sailed north to explore the Chesapeake Bay and the Potomac River. In 1614, he spent a summer on Monhegan Island, off the coast of Maine, and mapped the coast south to Cape Cod. He called the area New England, and his written descriptions of his travels interested investors of the Plymouth Company in England. This company would later finance the voyage of the Pilgrims. Smith's map of New England included a harbor called Patuxet, which would later be named Plymouth.

The Travels of Squanto

In 1614, another English sea captain, Thomas Hunt, kidnapped about twenty-seven Indians off the Massachusetts coast and took them to Spain, where they were sold as slaves. One of these men was a Patuxet Indian named Tisquantum, or Squanto. After about three years of servitude, either he was released or he escaped, and he traveled to England. There he was befriended by a merchant named John Slaney, who taught him to speak English. In 1619, Slaney arranged for Squanto to return to America. He traveled aboard an English ship to Newfoundland and from there made his way back to his home in Patuxet. Once a thriving center of the Wampanoag Confederacy, Patuxet was now deserted, its people wiped out by an epidemic of disease. Squanto, the last of the Patuxet Indians, went to live with a nearby Wampanoag tribe. The following year, the Pilgrims arrived to make their home at the site of the Patuxet village. Squanto would play an important role in their survival.

Index

Page numbers in *italics* refer to illustrations.